BOATS!
(and other things that float)

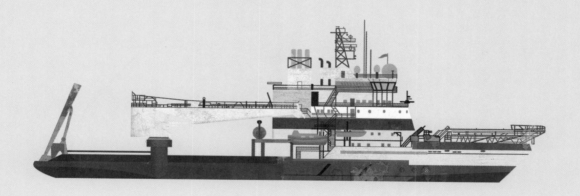

THIS IS A WELBECK CHILDREN'S BOOK

Published in 2021 by Welbeck Children's Books
An imprint of Welbeck Children's Limited, part of Welbeck Publishing Group
20 Mortimer Street, London W1T 3JW

Associate Publisher: Laura Knowles
Commissioning Editor: Bryony Davies
Art Editor: Deborah Vickers
Art Director: Margaret Hope
Designer: Dani Lurie
Production: Melanie Robertson

A CIP catalogue record for this book is available from
the British Library.

ISBN: 978-1-78312-640-8

Printed in Heshan, China

10 9 8 7 6 5 4 3 2 1

WELBECK

BOATS!
(and other things that float)

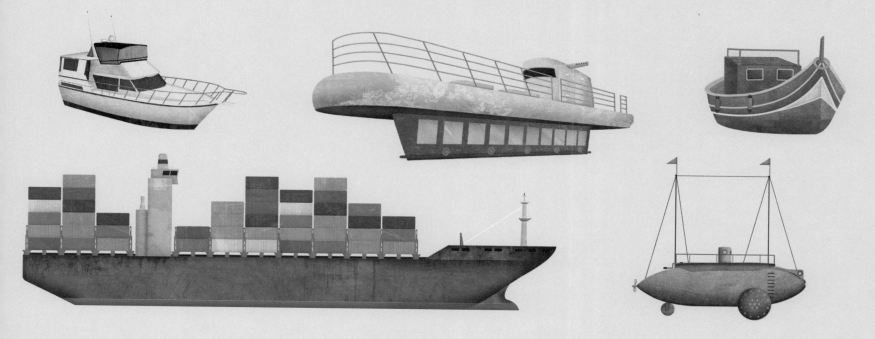

Written by Bryony Davies
and Catherine Veitch

Illustrated by
Maria Brzozowska

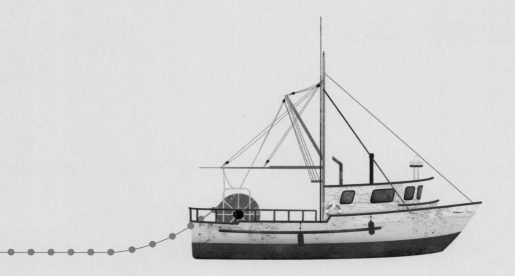

This book belongs to:

Contents

Let's Set Sail

Many boats are powered by the wind, which fills their sails and pushes them along. Sails come in different shapes and sizes; some boats just have one sail, and others have many.

Wendur

Trabaccolo

Felucca

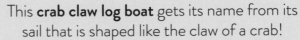

This **crab claw log boat** gets its name from its sail that is shaped like the claw of a crab!

This **Viking longship** was used in battles. It could quickly zip through the water because of its long, thin shape. If there was no wind it could be rowed.

Japanese wooden cargo boat

This gigantic **schooner** called *Thomas W Lawson* was the largest sailing ship when it was built. Sailors had to use motors to raise its huge sails!

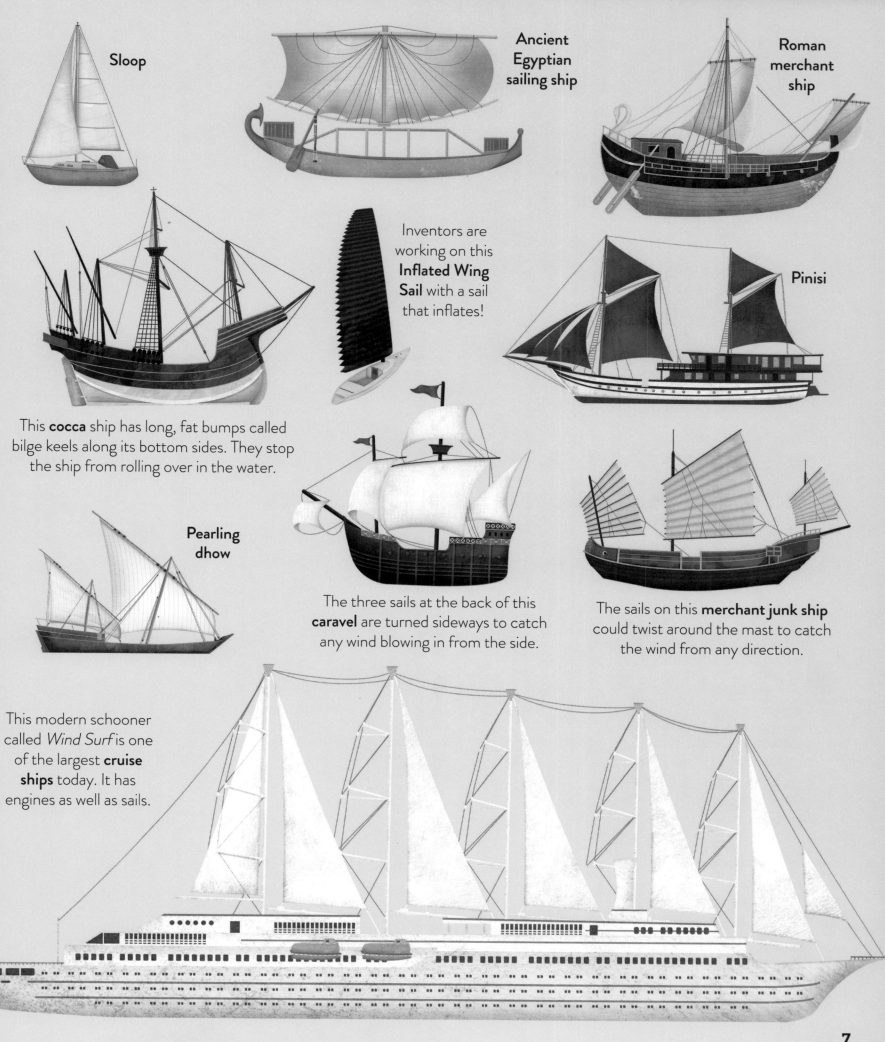

Sloop

Ancient Egyptian sailing ship

Roman merchant ship

Inventors are working on this **Inflated Wing Sail** with a sail that inflates!

Pinisi

This **cocca** ship has long, fat bumps called bilge keels along its bottom sides. They stop the ship from rolling over in the water.

Pearling dhow

The three sails at the back of this **caravel** are turned sideways to catch any wind blowing in from the side.

The sails on this **merchant junk ship** could twist around the mast to catch the wind from any direction.

This modern schooner called *Wind Surf* is one of the largest **cruise ships** today. It has engines as well as sails.

The Parts of a Boat

Boats float because they are buoyant. They are pushed up by the water beneath them. What are the **different parts of a boat called?**

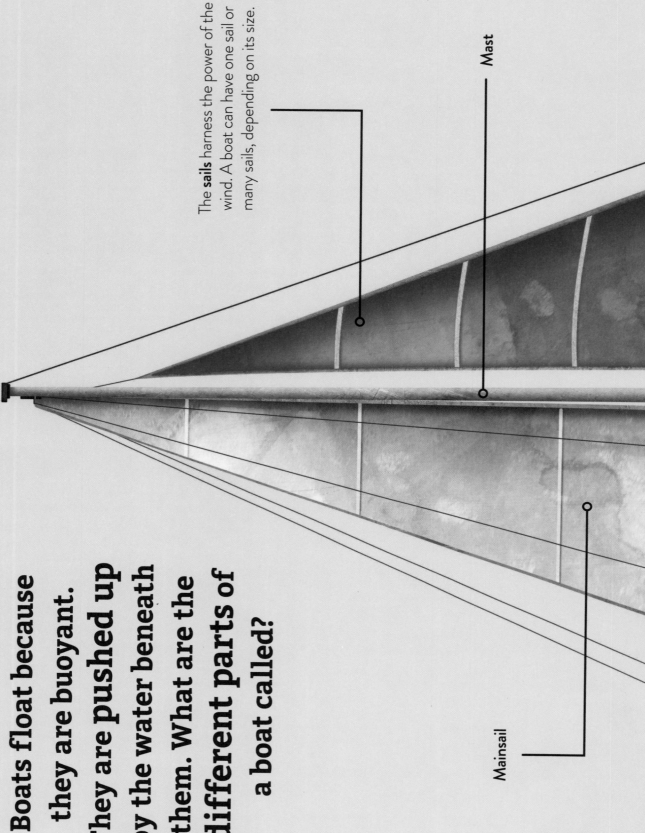

The **sails** harness the power of the wind. A boat can have one sail or many sails, depending on its size.

Mast

Mainsail

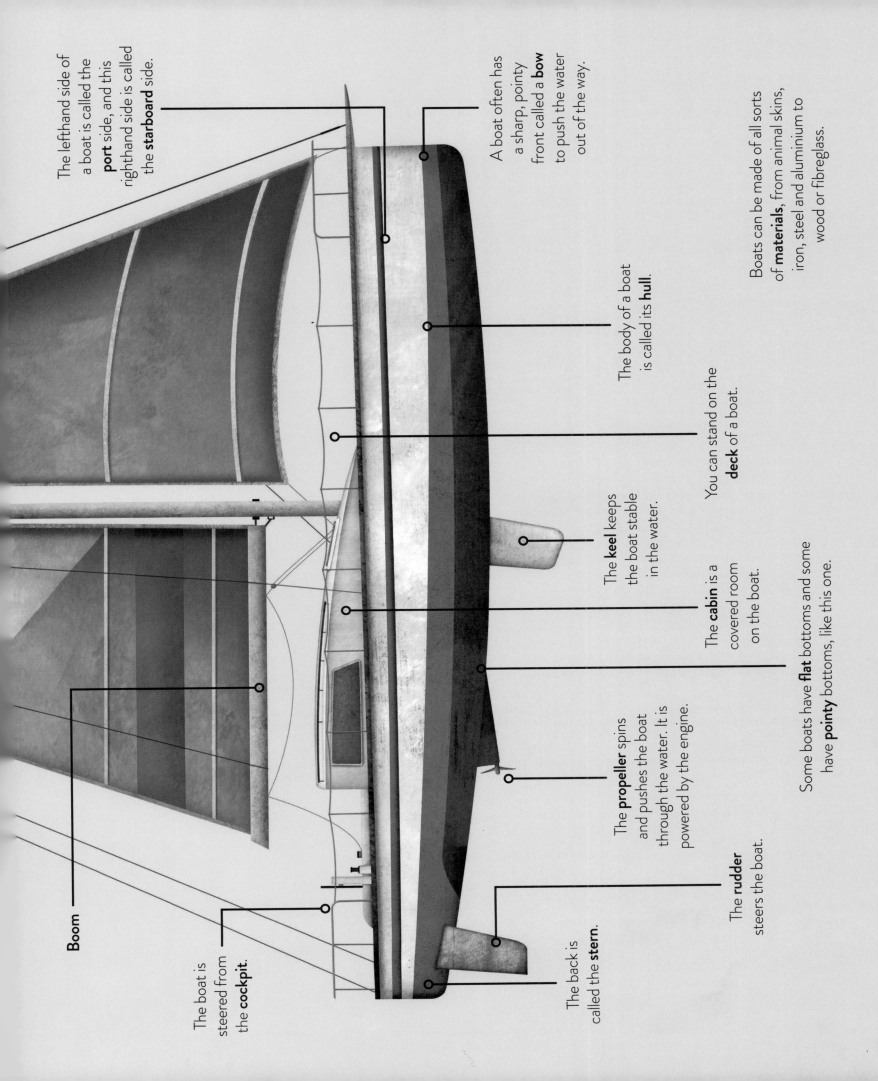

The lefthand side of a boat is called the **port** side, and this righthand side is called the **starboard** side.

A boat often has a sharp, pointy front called a **bow** to push the water out of the way.

Boats can be made of all sorts of **materials,** from animal skins, iron, steel and aluminium to wood or fibreglass.

The body of a boat is called its **hull**.

You can stand on the **deck** of a boat.

The **keel** keeps the boat stable in the water.

The **cabin** is a covered room on the boat.

Some boats have **flat** bottoms and some have **pointy** bottoms, like this one.

The **propeller** spins and pushes the boat through the water. It is powered by the engine.

Boom

The boat is steered from the **cockpit.**

The **rudder** steers the boat.

The back is called the **stern**.

Lifeboats to the Rescue

If you ever need to be helped out at sea, a lifeboat will come to your rescue. **Powerful** and **fast**, they help people in trouble.

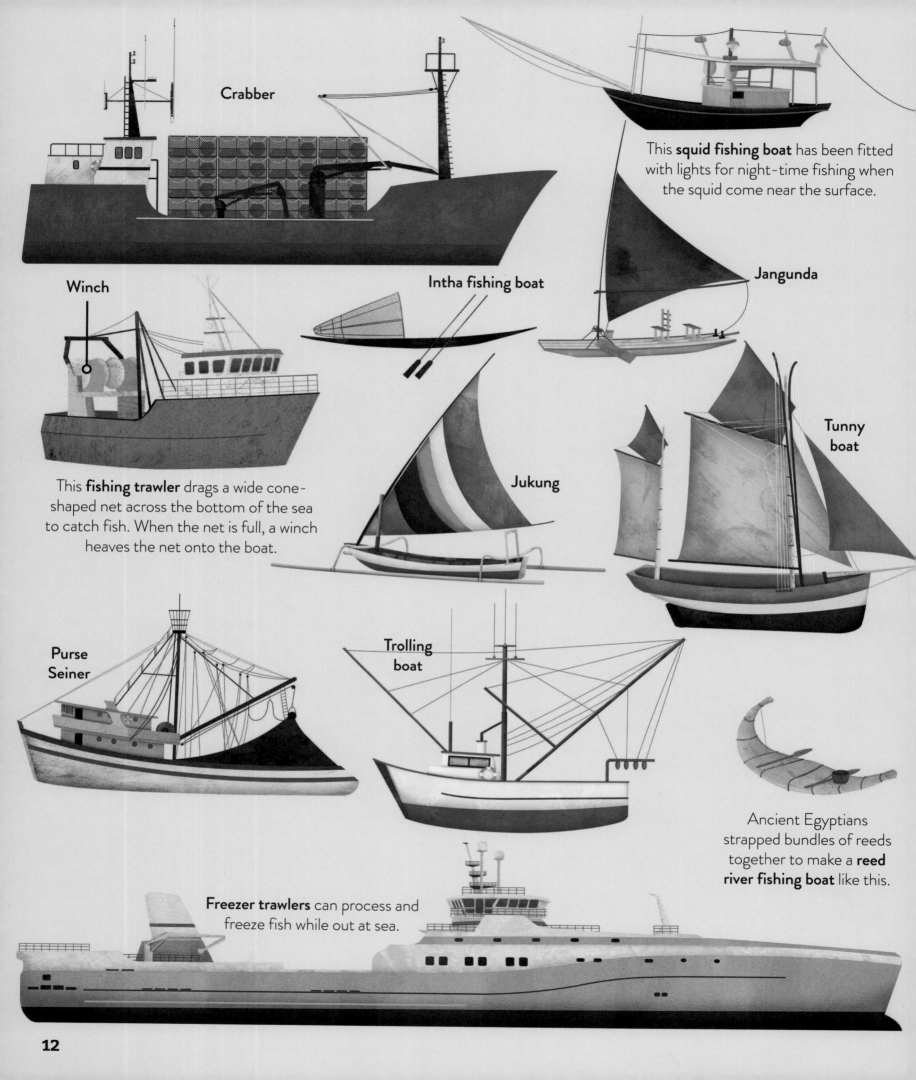

Crabber

This **squid fishing boat** has been fitted with lights for night-time fishing when the squid come near the surface.

Winch

Intha fishing boat

Jangunda

This **fishing trawler** drags a wide cone-shaped net across the bottom of the sea to catch fish. When the net is full, a winch heaves the net onto the boat.

Jukung

Tunny boat

Purse Seiner

Trolling boat

Ancient Egyptians strapped bundles of reeds together to make a **reed river fishing boat** like this.

Freezer trawlers can process and freeze fish while out at sea.

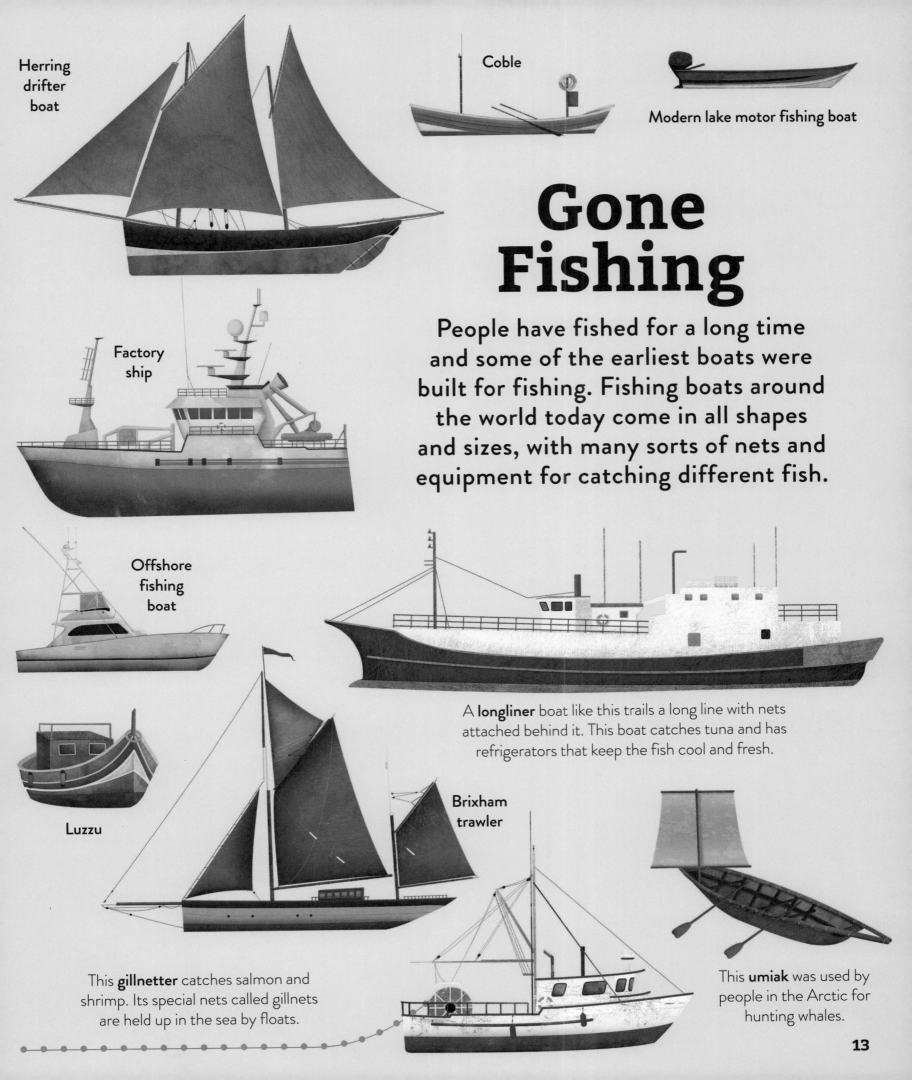

Herring drifter boat

Coble

Modern lake motor fishing boat

Gone Fishing

People have fished for a long time and some of the earliest boats were built for fishing. Fishing boats around the world today come in all shapes and sizes, with many sorts of nets and equipment for catching different fish.

Factory ship

Offshore fishing boat

Luzzu

Brixham trawler

A **longliner** boat like this trails a long line with nets attached behind it. This boat catches tuna and has refrigerators that keep the fish cool and fresh.

This **gillnetter** catches salmon and shrimp. Its special nets called gillnets are held up in the sea by floats.

This **umiak** was used by people in the Arctic for hunting whales.

Boats moor up to anchored
floating balls called buoys.

Time to unload
today's catch.

Fishing
nets

14

At the Fishing Harbour

The fishing harbour is a **busy, bustling place.**
Boats chug in and out, landing their catches
of fish, crabs or lobsters. Seagulls hover in the
breeze, hoping for a bite to eat.

This fishing boat is
setting off out to sea,
ready to catch some fish.

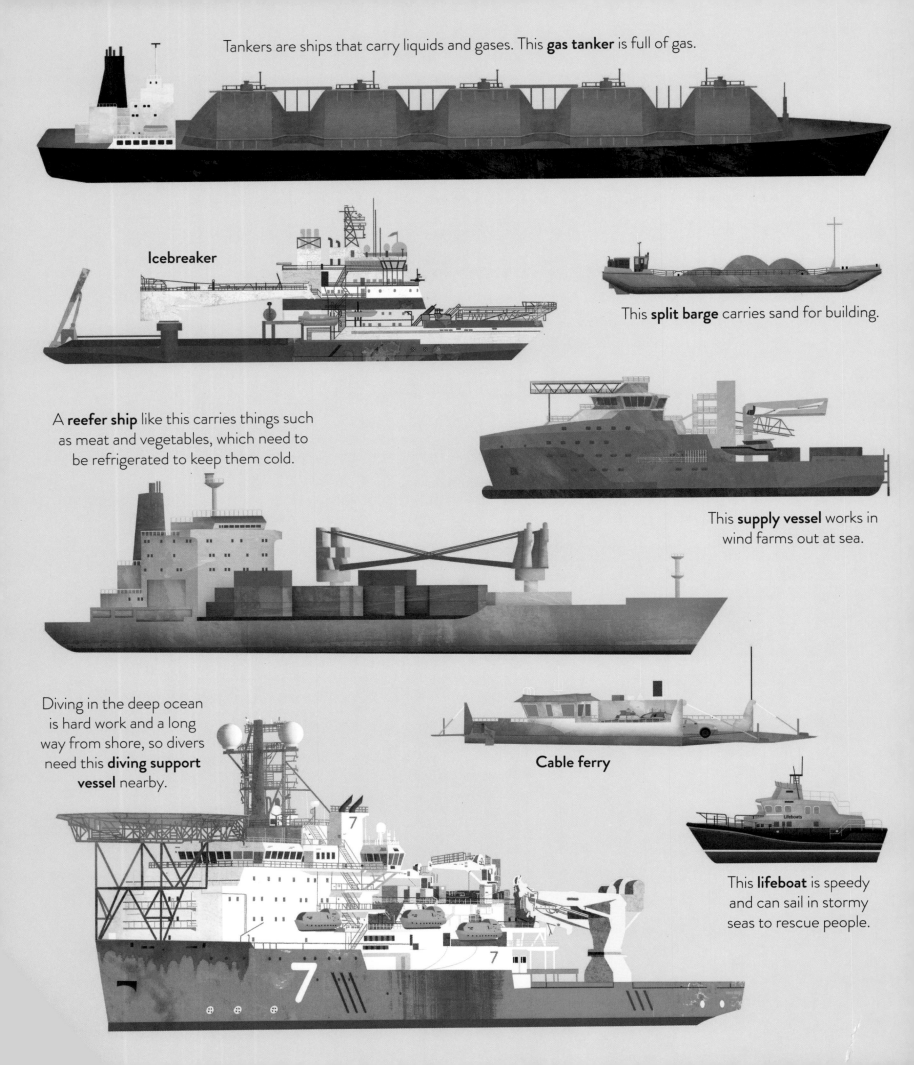

Tankers are ships that carry liquids and gases. This **gas tanker** is full of gas.

Icebreaker

This **split barge** carries sand for building.

A **reefer ship** like this carries things such as meat and vegetables, which need to be refrigerated to keep them cold.

This **supply vessel** works in wind farms out at sea.

Diving in the deep ocean is hard work and a long way from shore, so divers need this **diving support vessel** nearby.

Cable ferry

This **lifeboat** is speedy and can sail in stormy seas to rescue people.

Fireboat

River taxi

Hard at Work

Every day thousands of boats are hard at work in different ways, which include carrying people and materials across seas and along rivers, helping other boats and even saving lives.

Huge **container ships** like this carry goods. The goods are stored in truck-size containers that can be lifted off the ship and put onto a truck.

Water ambulance

Police patrol boat

Sprague was the largest **steam towboat** ever built. The mighty ship pushed barges up river, and set a record for pushing 60 barges at once!

A **tugboat** helps out ships at sea by pushing them, or pulling them with a tug line. The ships may be stuck in a tight canal or broken down.

Oil or chemical tanker

Tugboats have powerful engines and special propellers to help them move ships that are much larger than they are.

Towing Tugboats

Tugboats are small but powerful boats that can push and pull ships that are a lot bigger than them. These tugboats are guiding a large ship into harbour.

They connect to the larger ships using strong cables.

The tugs don't just steer larger boats, they can also help to slow them down.

This **bucentaur** belonged to the ruler of Venice.

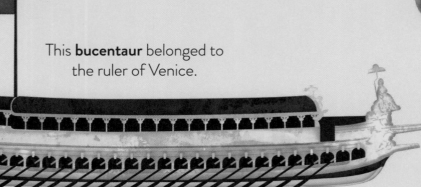

This **dugout canoe** was made by hollowing out a large tree trunk.

Fishing raft

Modern wooden rowing boat

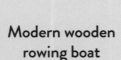

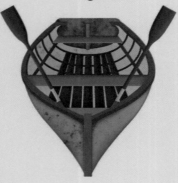

Heave-Ho, Make it Go!

Rowers need plenty of puff to move rowing boats through the water using oars. Some of the first boats were rowing boats.

The **Thung-chai** is nicknamed a 'basket boat' because it is made by weaving bamboo.

This huge **Khufu barge** was made long ago by the ancient Egyptians.

A gondolier stands up in this **gondola** and pushes it along with a long oar.

The float on the side of this **outrigger canoe** helps to keep the boat steady in choppy seas.

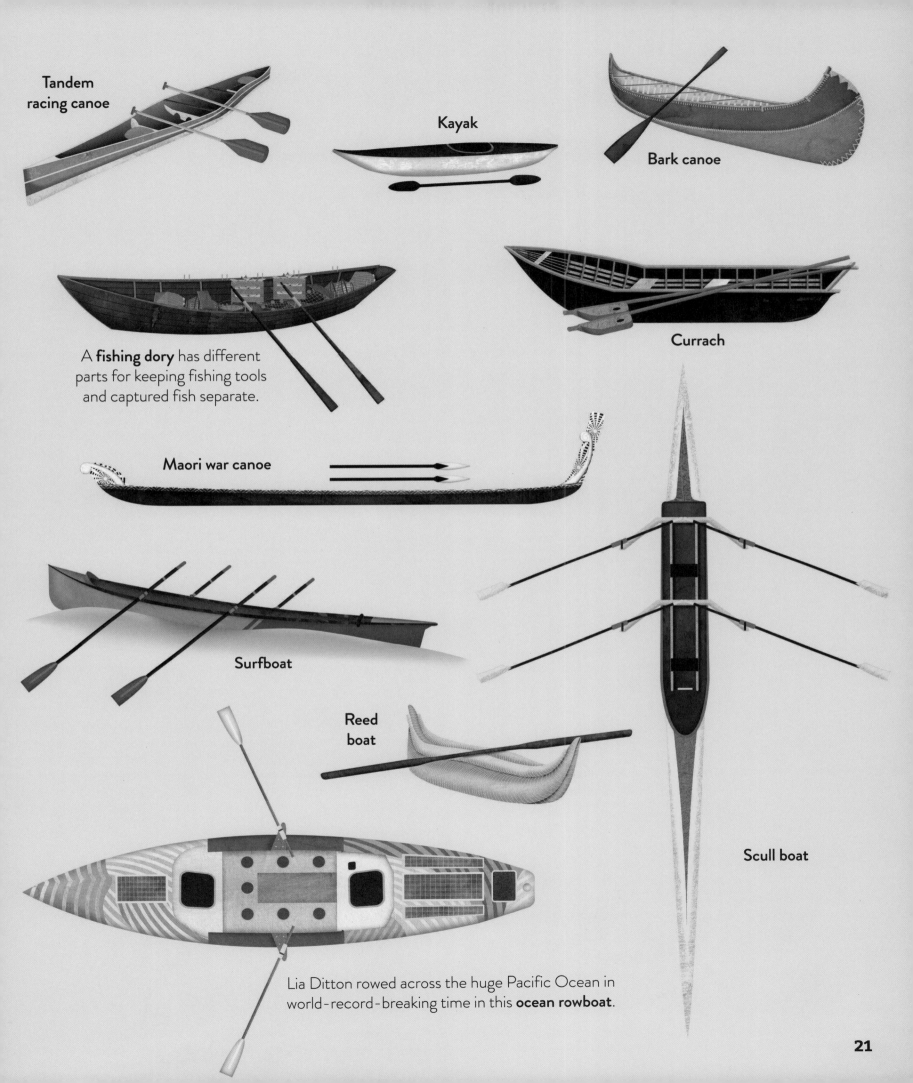

Tandem racing canoe

Kayak

Bark canoe

A **fishing dory** has different parts for keeping fishing tools and captured fish separate.

Currach

Maori war canoe

Surfboat

Reed boat

Scull boat

Lia Ditton rowed across the huge Pacific Ocean in world-record-breaking time in this **ocean rowboat**.

Ready, Steady, Race!

It's a dragon boat race! These long, narrow rowing boats are shaped like dragons, and originally come from China. They are **really fun** to race.

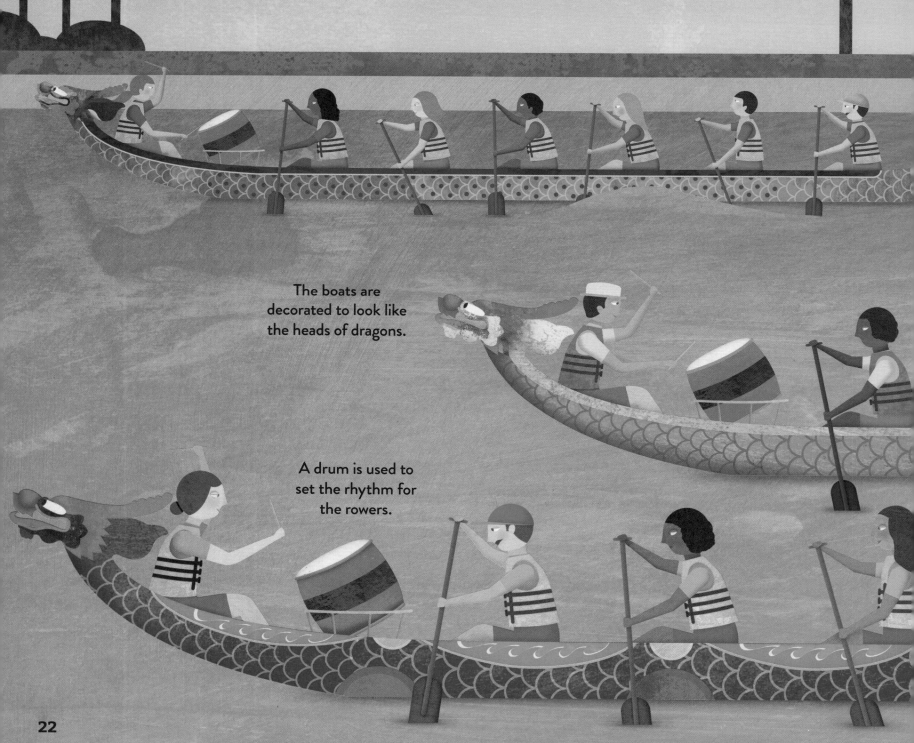

The boats are decorated to look like the heads of dragons.

A drum is used to set the rhythm for the rowers.

Teams row as fast as they
can to see who will win.

This huge **passenger liner**, the RMS *Titanic*, was built over a hundred years ago and carried over 2,000 passengers and 1,000 crew. Sadly she sank on her first voyage.

Houseboat

This is called a **ro-ro ferry** because cars **ro**ll on and **ro**ll off.

Water bus

This huge **cruise ship**, the *Allure of the Seas*, has eight decks, a basketball court, ice-skating rink and 14 pools!

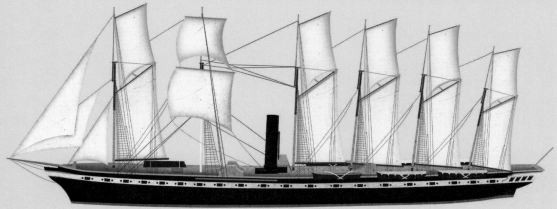

A powerful steam engine works with the sails to drive this mighty iron **passenger steamship**, the SS *Great Britain*.

People live on **narrowboats**. There isn't much room inside, but most include a bed, somewhere to sit and eat, a kitchen, and even a shower and a toilet!

All Aboard

Hundreds of people travel along rivers and across oceans on boats. They might take a holiday on a cruise ship, travel for work, or even call a boat their home.

River steamboat

Hydrofoil

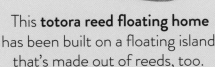

This **totora reed floating home** has been built on a floating island that's made out of reeds, too.

Houseboat

This **floating home** in Canada is in a village of floating homes.

Paddle steamships like the *Savannah* had a paddlewheel.

Bigger **steamship liners** like this SS *Kaiser Wilhelm Der Grosse* were built to carry more passengers. They had more engines and more funnels to power them.

A Day on the Canal

Long, narrow boats potter slowly up the canal.
They stop to go through locks, waiting patiently
as the **water rises**, before they set off again.

Some people live on canal
boats, and other people like to
hire them for holidays.

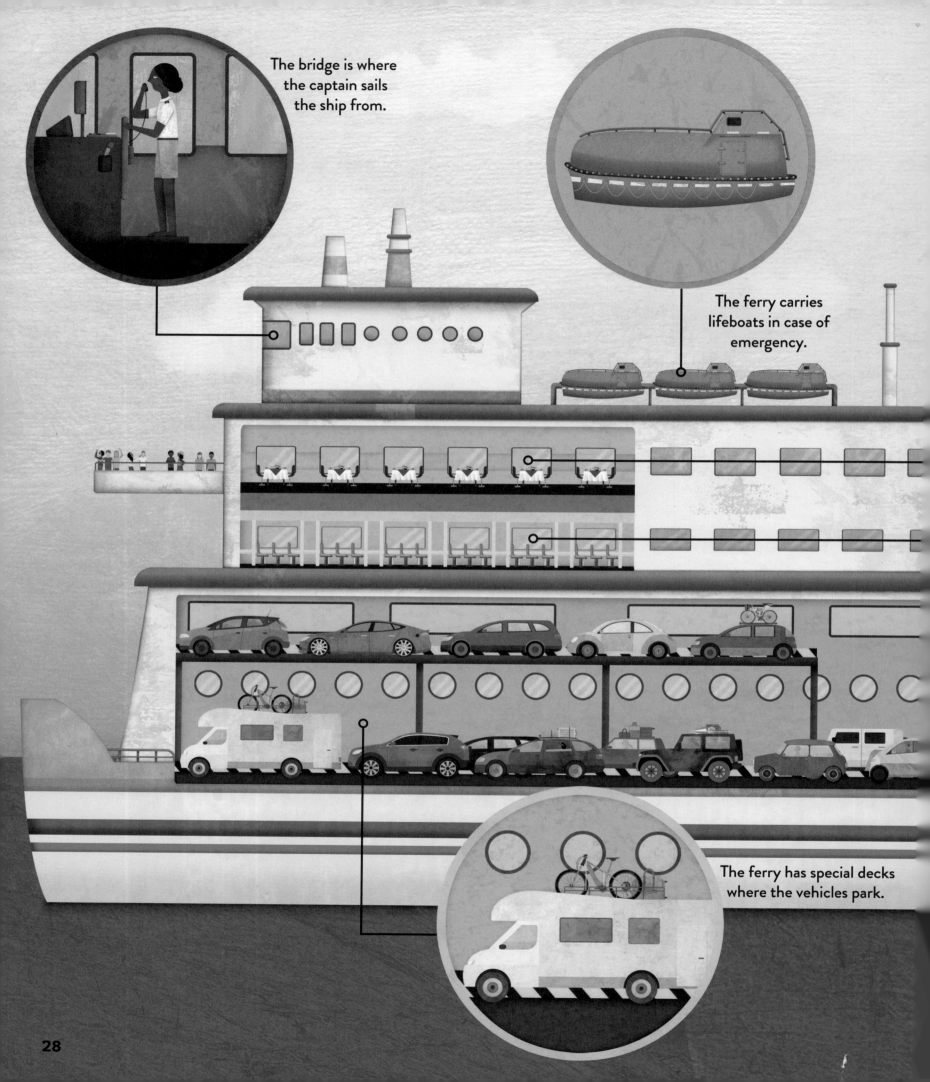

The bridge is where the captain sails the ship from.

The ferry carries lifeboats in case of emergency.

The ferry has special decks where the vehicles park.

Inside a Car Ferry

Car ferries can be loaded up with cars and all sorts of vehicles, to take them **across the water** on holiday, or even just to work.

There's somewhere to have a bite to eat.

Passengers can leave their vehicles and enjoy their journey, relaxing in the passenger lounges.

Vehicles can drive on to the ferry using the large ramp.

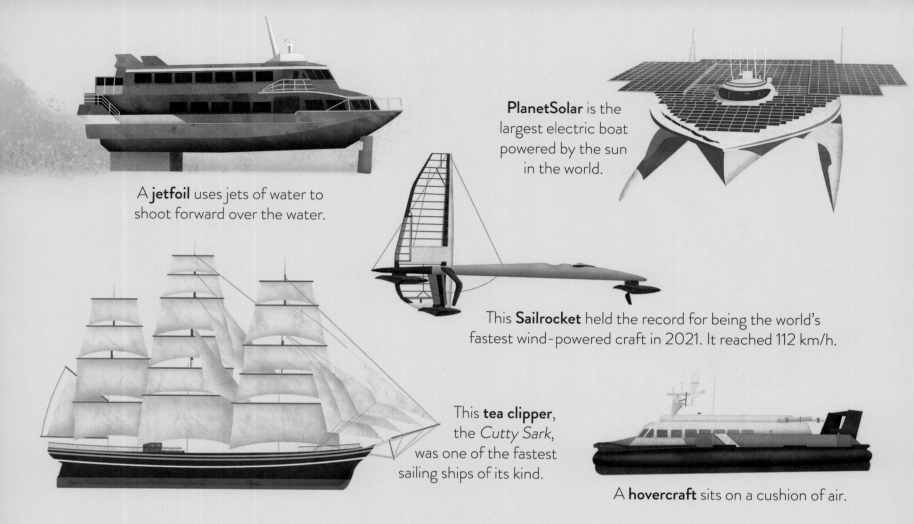

A **jetfoil** uses jets of water to shoot forward over the water.

PlanetSolar is the largest electric boat powered by the sun in the world.

This **Sailrocket** held the record for being the world's fastest wind-powered craft in 2021. It reached 112 km/h.

This **tea clipper**, the *Cutty Sark*, was one of the fastest sailing ships of its kind.

A **hovercraft** sits on a cushion of air.

Record Breakers

People have discovered different ways of making boats better and faster by changing their shape, the materials they are made from, how they are powered, and even lifting the boat up out of the water. Here are some record-breaking boats.

This is one of the **largest cruise ships** in the world with 18 decks, 22 restaurants, 24 pools and 2,759 cabins!

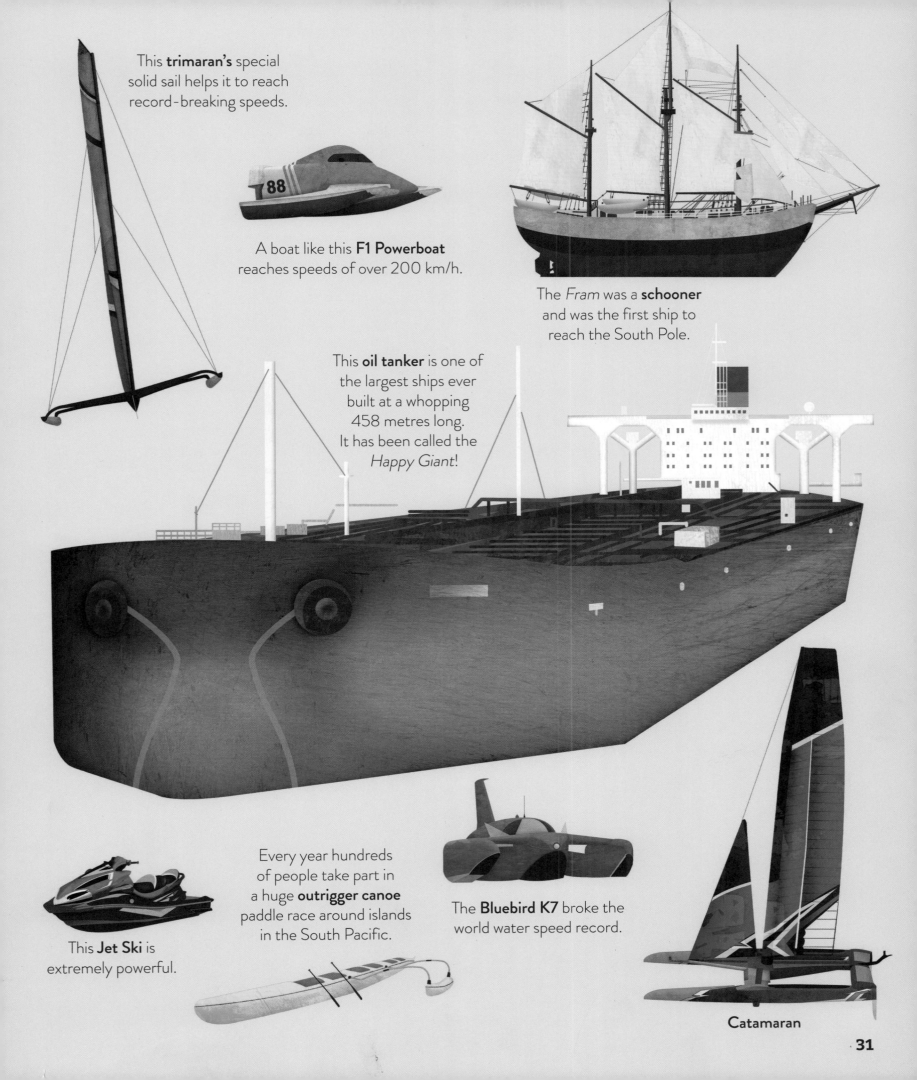

This **trimaran's** special solid sail helps it to reach record-breaking speeds.

A boat like this **F1 Powerboat** reaches speeds of over 200 km/h.

The *Fram* was a **schooner** and was the first ship to reach the South Pole.

This **oil tanker** is one of the largest ships ever built at a whopping 458 metres long. It has been called the *Happy Giant*!

Every year hundreds of people take part in a huge **outrigger canoe** paddle race around islands in the South Pacific.

The **Bluebird K7** broke the world water speed record.

This **Jet Ski** is extremely powerful.

Catamaran

Loading Up at the Port

Goods **large and small**, from toys to cars – and even this book – are carried **across the world** by ship. They are loaded up and taken off the ships at busy docks.

These cargo ships are called RORO ships. The cargo they carry, such as cars, can roll on and roll off easily.

Deck boat

This **bow rider** has extra seats at the front, or the bow, for people to enjoy the ride.

Air boat

This **racing kayak** seats two people.

Semi sub

Every year people in Kerala, India race these magnificent **snake boats**. Up to 100 people can be in each boat!

White water rafting in an **inflatable river raft** like this can be hair-raising!

Motor yacht

This **windsurf** needs a windy day to push it along.

Sit on this giant, inflatable **banana boat** and be pulled along by another boat for an exciting ride.

Fun pool inflatable

People in Taiwan race these **dragon boats** in a three-day festival. The fun has caught on and many people around the world also race dragon boats.

Water scooter

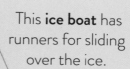

This **ice boat** has runners for sliding over the ice.

Time for Fun

It can be great fun on the water. Have you ever pedalled hard with your feet to make a pedalo go, or ridden an inflatable flamingo?

Motorboat

There is room to sleep on a **cabin cruiser**!

It takes a lot of practise to balance on a **paddleboard**!

At the Floating Market

Boats are laden with all kinds of fruit to buy.

Tasty smells fill the air as vendors cook fresh food to sell on their boats.

It's time to shop at the market with a difference – **it floats!** A crowd of boats gathers, selling anything you could possibly need to buy, from fruit and vegetables to hats.

Traffic jam! The market is bustling and busy.

Would you like to buy an umbrella, or perhaps a hat?

Super Submarines

Boats called submarines can travel underwater!
Early submarines were used in battles, but today
submarines are also built for different things such as
exploring the deep ocean and for leisure.

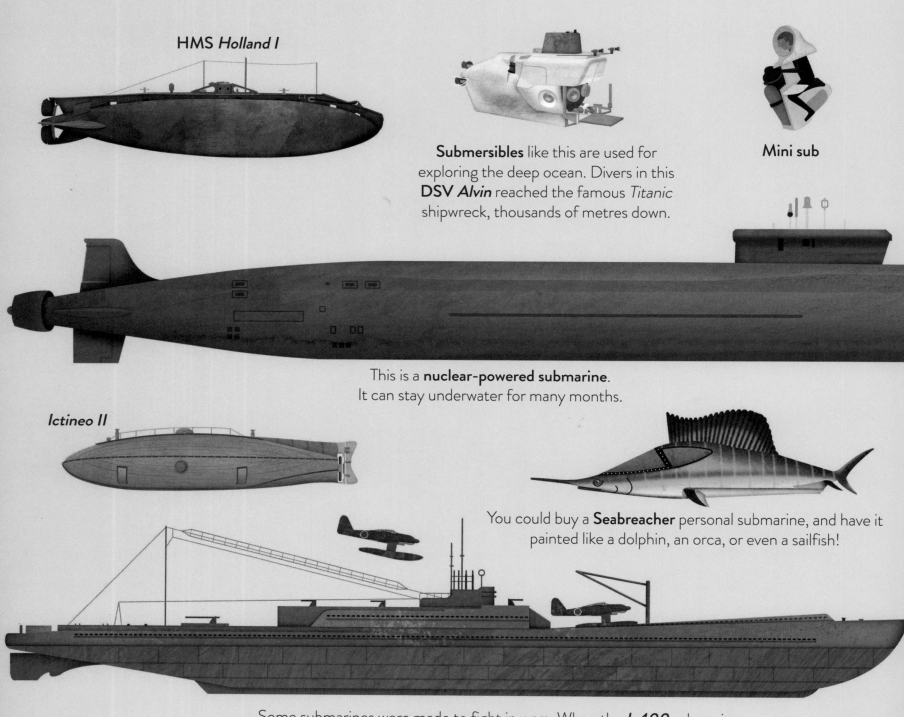

HMS *Holland I*

Submersibles like this are used for exploring the deep ocean. Divers in this **DSV** *Alvin* reached the famous *Titanic* shipwreck, thousands of metres down.

Mini sub

This is a **nuclear-powered submarine**.
It can stay underwater for many months.

Ictineo II

You could buy a **Seabreacher** personal submarine, and have it painted like a dolphin, an orca, or even a sailfish!

Some submarines were made to fight in wars. When the *I-400* submarine was at the surface, planes could land and take off from its deck.

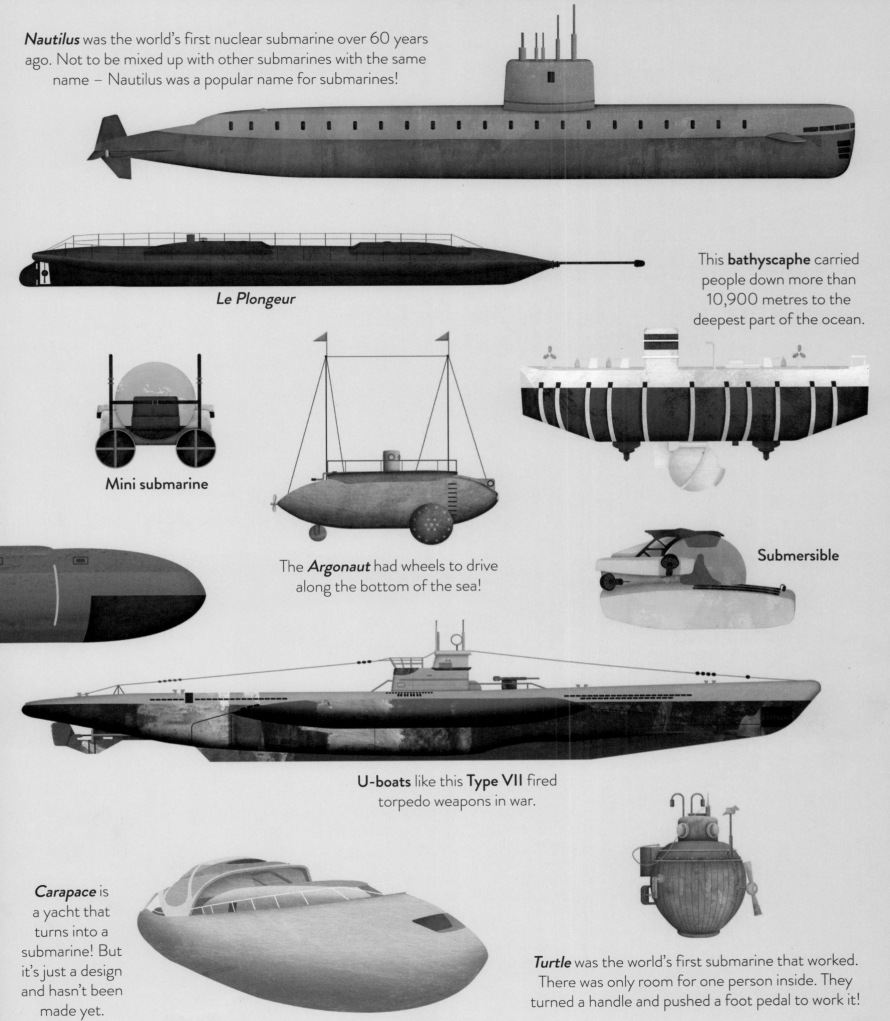

Nautilus was the world's first nuclear submarine over 60 years ago. Not to be mixed up with other submarines with the same name – Nautilus was a popular name for submarines!

Le Plongeur

This **bathyscaphe** carried people down more than 10,900 metres to the deepest part of the ocean.

Mini submarine

The *Argonaut* had wheels to drive along the bottom of the sea!

Submersible

U-boats like this **Type VII** fired torpedo weapons in war.

Carapace is a yacht that turns into a submarine! But it's just a design and hasn't been made yet.

Turtle was the world's first submarine that worked. There was only room for one person inside. They turned a handle and pushed a foot pedal to work it!

Inside a Submarine

Large submarines generate their own power and can remain underwater for a long time, some up to 120 days. They have space for more than a hundred crewmembers to work, eat and sleep.

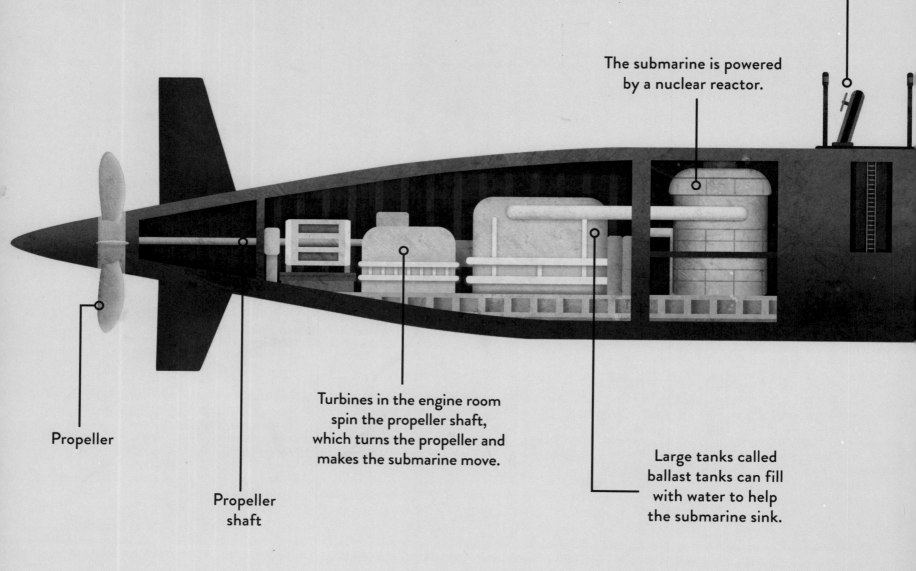

The crew enter and exit the submarine through a small hatch, and use ladders to climb between different levels.

The submarine is powered by a nuclear reactor.

Propeller

Propeller shaft

Turbines in the engine room spin the propeller shaft, which turns the propeller and makes the submarine move.

Large tanks called ballast tanks can fill with water to help the submarine sink.

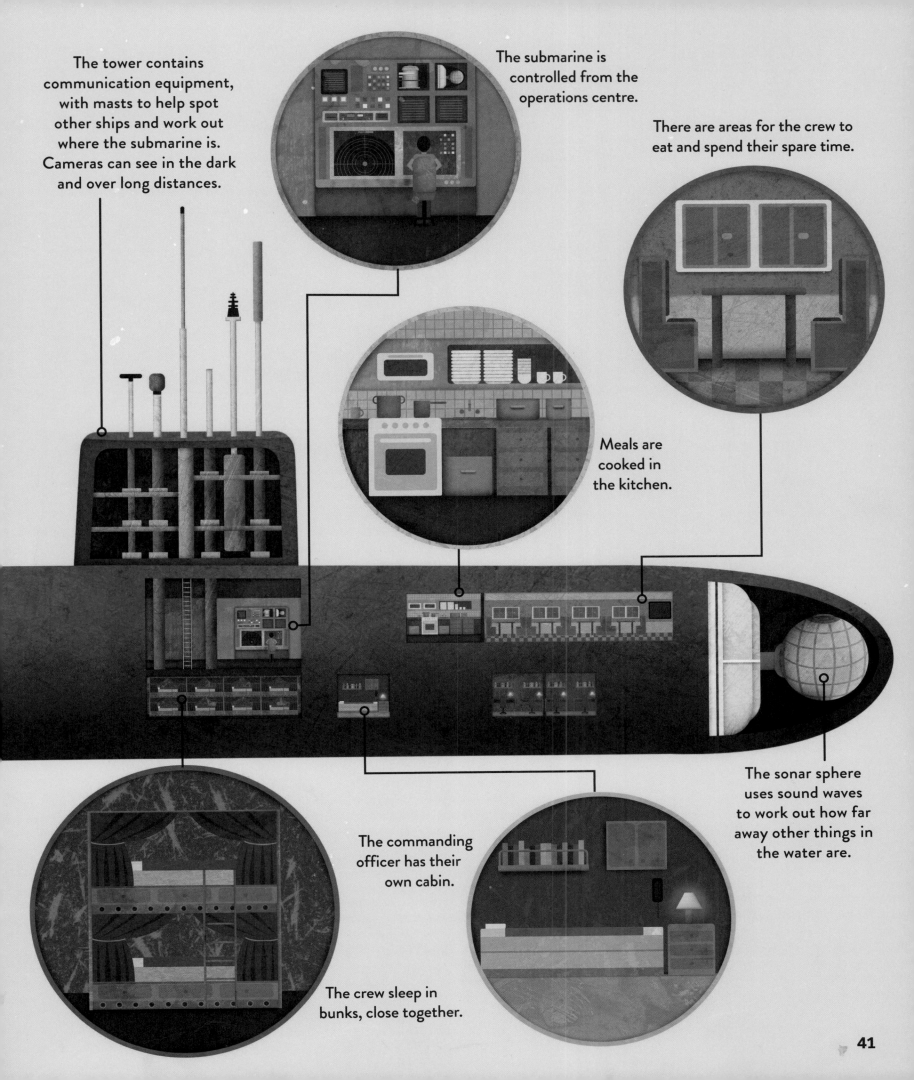

The tower contains communication equipment, with masts to help spot other ships and work out where the submarine is. Cameras can see in the dark and over long distances.

The submarine is controlled from the operations centre.

There are areas for the crew to eat and spend their spare time.

Meals are cooked in the kitchen.

The sonar sphere uses sound waves to work out how far away other things in the water are.

The commanding officer has their own cabin.

The crew sleep in bunks, close together.

Bismarck battleship

USS *Cairo* steam warship

The giant bowl-like parts on the deck of this **modern warship, *Monge* (A601),** track satellites and rockets.

This **amphibious warfare vessel** carries helicopters.

HMS *Dreadnought* battleship

The narrow body of a **Spanish galleon** meant it could race through the water.

P34 Patrol boat

Aircraft carrier, *Akagi*

The ***Mary Rose*** was a warship that belonged to King Henry VIII of England over 400 years ago.

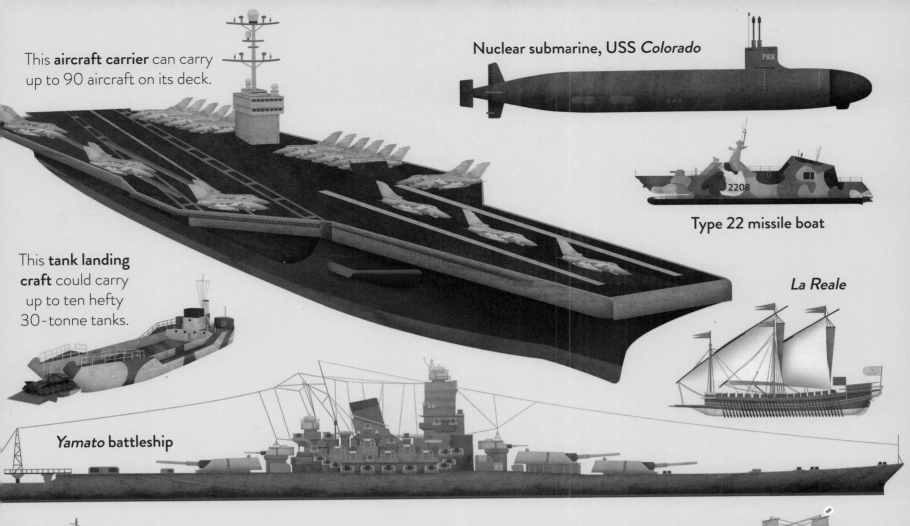

This **aircraft carrier** can carry up to 90 aircraft on its deck.

Nuclear submarine, USS *Colorado*

Type 22 missile boat

This **tank landing craft** could carry up to ten hefty 30-tonne tanks.

La Reale

Yamato battleship

Military Boats

Throughout time, people have fought battles at sea. Some are fought using small, fast boats. Other warships are mighty boats that can carry aircraft, troops and tanks. Some ships even spy on others.

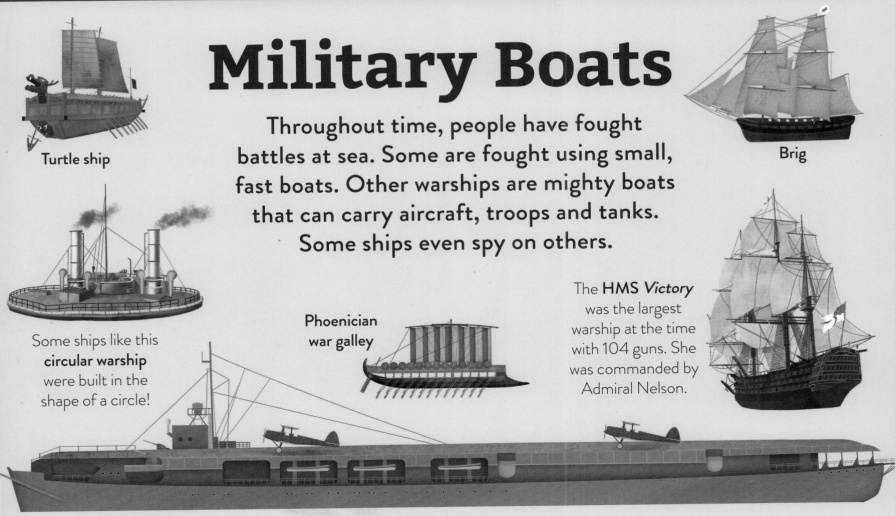

Turtle ship

Brig

Some ships like this **circular warship** were built in the shape of a circle!

Phoenician war galley

The **HMS** *Victory* was the largest warship at the time with 104 guns. She was commanded by Admiral Nelson.

Escort carrier, *Empire McAlpine*

Fun Floating Facts

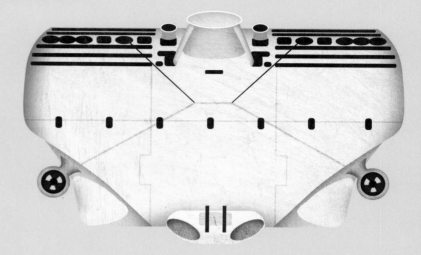

1. The deepest dive ever in a submarine was 10,927 metres, in a sub called DSV *Limiting Factor*.

2. Whistling on board a boat is thought to be bad luck as some people think it might bring strong winds. Cats are considered lucky to have on a ship, but bananas aren't.

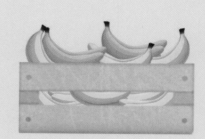

3. The toilet on board a ship is called the head.

4. Some cruise ships have robot waiters that can bring you a drink.

5. The world's busiest port is Shanghai in China. It handles more than 43,000 containers full of goods a year.

6. When sailing, speed is measured in knots. A knot is one nautical mile an hour.

7. Viking longships could sail across seas but also travel up shallow rivers because they had flat bottoms, so did not need to be in deep water.

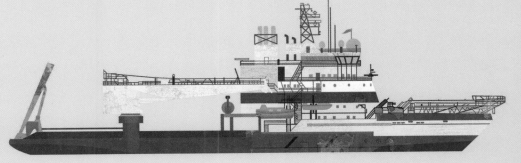

8. Some icebreaker ships are so strong that they can break through ice that is five metres thick.

9. Dazzle camouflage, or 'razzle dazzle', is a way of painting a ship in different colours and in geometric shapes, which makes it hard to see how fast it is travelling.

10. In 1992, around 29,000 rubber ducks escaped from a ship in the Pacific Ocean and floated all around the world.

Can You Spot?

Take a look through the book and see which of these things you can find!

Houseboat

Drummer

Helicopter

Fishing nets

Lighthouse

Two cormorants

Car with a bicycle on top

Coble

Sand

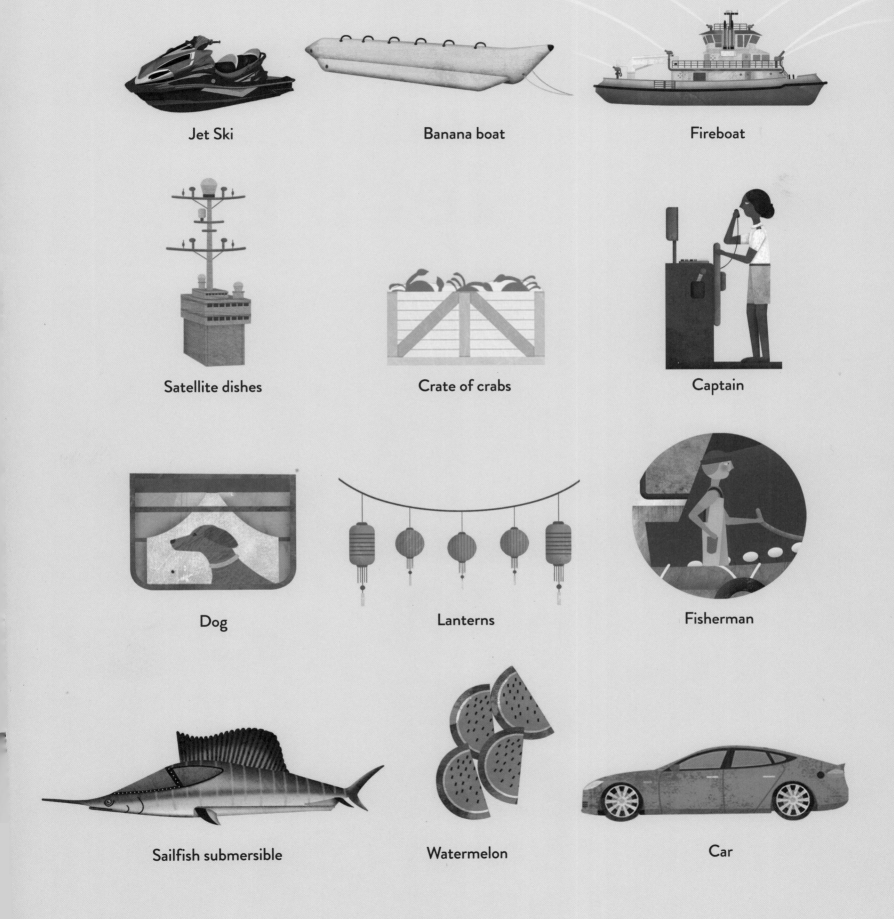

Jet Ski

Banana boat

Fireboat

Satellite dishes

Crate of crabs

Captain

Dog

Lanterns

Fisherman

Sailfish submersible

Watermelon

Car